2495

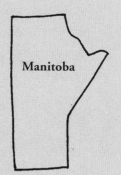

Manitoba

New
Brunswick

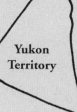

Yukon
Territory

British
Columbia

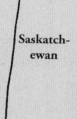

Alberta

Saskatch-
ewan

Cc

is for
Canada

Written by Vicki Berger Erwin   Illustrated by Mark Thurman

Published by GHB Publishers

GHB Publishers
3906 Old Highway 94 South, Suite 300
St. Charles, MO 63304

Book cover design by Werremeyer|Floresca
Cover illustration by Michelle Dorenkamp

Manufactured in the United States of America
First Edition

10 9 8 7 6 5 4 3 2 1

Library of Congress Cataloging-in-Publication Data

Erwin, Vicki Berger, 1951-
C is for Canada / by Vicki Berger Erwin, illustrated by Mark Thurman
Saint Charles, Mo : GHB Publishers, c2000.
60 p. : col. ill., maps ; 28 cm.
"Alpha Flight books"

Summary: An alphabetical introduction to the history, geography,
culture, industries, and recreations of Canada.

1. English language--Alphabet--Juvenile literature.
2. Alphabet.
3. Canada--Juvenile literature.
4. Canada.

I. Thurman, Mark, ill.
II. Series
III. Title.

F1008.2   2000   971--dc21

ISBN 1-892920-30-1

"A" is for the Arctic • "B" is for Beaver • "C" is for Canada Day • "D" is for Dinosaur • "E" is for Explorer • "F" is for French Heritage • "G" is for Glacier • "H" is for Hockey • "I" is for the Inuit • "J" is for Jasper National Park • "K" is for "Kanata" • "L" is for Lumberjack • "M" is for Maple Leaf • "N" is for Niagara Falls • "O" is for the Olympics • "P" is for Polar Bear • "Q" is for Queen Elizabeth II • "R" is for the Royal Canadian Mounted Police • "S" is for Stampede • "T" is for the Trans-Canada Highway • "U" is for the Underground Railroad • "V" i[s ...] '67 • "Y" is for the Yukon • "Z" [...] aver • "C" is for Canada Day • [...] " is for French Heritage • "G" [...] Inuit • "J" is for Jasper Nation[...] ack • "M" is for Maple Leaf • "N" is for Niagara Falls • "O" is for the Olympics • "P" is for Polar Bear • "Q" is for Queen Elizabeth II • "R" is for the Royal Canadian Mounted Police • "S" is for Stampede • "T" is for the Trans-Canada Highway • "U" is for the Underground Railroad • "V" is for Viking • "W" is for Whale • "X" is for Expo '67 • "Y" is for the Yukon • "Z" is for Zoo • "A" is for the Arctic • "B" is for Beaver • "C" is for Canada Day • "D" is for Dinosaur • "E" is for Explorer • "F" is for French Heritage • "G" is for Glacier • "H" is for Hockey • "I" is for

For Andy, Jordan, Kyle, and Sarah
— V.B.E.

For all Canadians who work towards tolerance and understanding
— M.T.

CANADA NATIONAL SYMBOLS

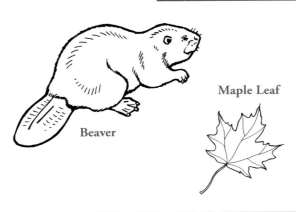

Beaver

Maple Leaf

Maple Tree

Canadian Flag

CANADA PROVINCES AND TERRITORIES/CAPITALS

Alberta/Edmonton
British Columbia/Victoria
Manitoba/Winnipeg
New Brunswick/Fredericton
Newfoundland/St. John's

Northwest Territories/Yellowknife
Nova Scotia/Halifax
Nunavut/Iqaluit
Ontario/Toronto
Prince Edward Island/Charlottetown

Quebec/Quebec
Saskatchewan/Regina
Yukon Territory/Whitehorse

Capital of Canada: Ottawa, Ontario

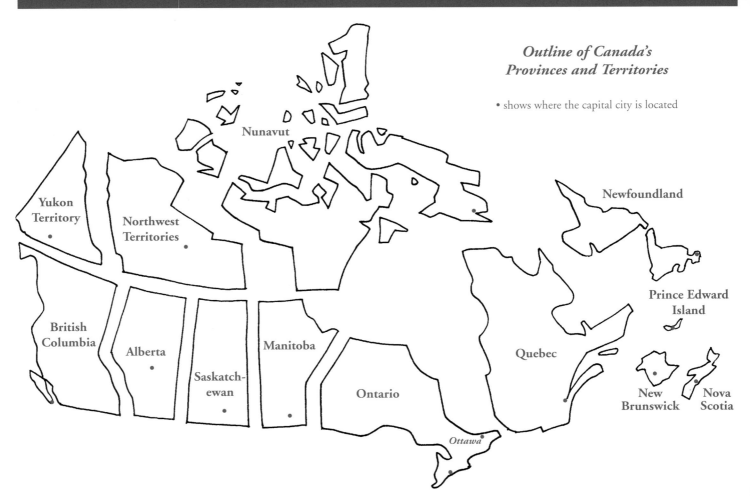

Outline of Canada's Provinces and Territories

• shows where the capital city is located

Nunavut

Yukon Territory

Northwest Territories

Newfoundland

British Columbia

Alberta

Saskatch-ewan

Manitoba

Ontario

Quebec

Prince Edward Island

New Brunswick

Nova Scotia

Ottawa

CANADA history

Canada is the second largest country in the world, stretching over 9,970, 610 square kilometers (3,849,674 square miles). Approximately 28,346,761 people live in Canada.

The first people to settle in Canada are known today as the First Nations. Each of the nations has its own language and culture. The Inuit, another group of original settlers, came to live in Canada's Arctic regions over 5,000 years ago.

In 1000 A.D., the Vikings were the first Europeans to visit Canadian shores. They settled briefly in Newfoundland.

John Cabot discovered the rich fishing grounds off the coast of Newfoundland in 1497. He was looking for the Northwest Passage. He made a second trip to the New World in 1498 and was never heard from again.

Jacques Cartier claimed Canada for France in 1534. He was also the first person to call the country Canada. The name may be based on the Huron/Iroquois word "kanata," which means village. He was also looking for the Northwest Passage.

In 1583, Sir Humphrey Gilbert claimed Newfoundland for England. The French and English lived together in Canada until the French and Indian War. In 1763, France gave up its land to England.

The provinces banded together as the Dominion of Canada in 1867. Canada became independent of Great Britain in 1931, although they still share a common monarch.

Today Canada is made up of ten provinces and three territories. The newest territory is Nunavut, created in 1999.

The main industries in Canada are agriculture, fishing, forestry, mining, and manufacturing.

The people of Canada come from many different backgrounds. Most of them live in cities in the southern part of the country.

The capital of Canada is Ottawa, Ontario. Other large cities are Toronto, Ontario; Montreal, Quebec; Calgary, Alberta; and Vancouver, British Columbia. Canada has two official languages: French and English.

AAa is for the Arctic.

Part of Canada is located north of the Arctic Circle.

4

In winter in the Arctic, the nights can last all day. In summer, the days can last all night. Few people live in the Arctic regions of Canada. But there are many animals in the Arctic, including polar bears, arctic foxes, musk oxen, and birds.

BBb is for beaver.

The beaver is a Canadian national symbol.

One of the reasons Europeans settled in Canada was to trade furs. Fur hats were popular in the 1700s. By the 1800s, the beaver was close to extinction. Today, thanks to conservation, Canada's largest rodent is alive and well all over the country.

 **is for Canada Day.**

Canada Day is a national holiday of Canada. It is celebrated every year on July 1.
It marks the date in 1867 when Upper and Lower Canada became one country. Before 1982, Canada Day was known as Dominion Day.

Dd

is for
dinosaur.

Dinosaurs roamed Canada when it was warm and swampy.

10

Today some of the richest fossil beds in the world are located in the Drumheller Badlands in Alberta. This area includes Dinosaur Provincial Park and the Royal Tyrrell Museum. There are more complete dinosaur skeletons displayed in Dinosaur Hall at the Royal Tyrrell Museum than anyplace in the world.

Overview of the Drumheller Badlands.

E

Ee

is for

explorer.

Explorers looking for the Northwest Passage (a shorter way between Europe and the Far East)

John Cabot sighting New Found Land, 1497.

landed in Canada. John Cabot, sailing for England, landed in Canada in 1497. In 1534, Jacques Cartier claimed Canada for France.

Ff is for French heritage.

The French were early settlers in Canada. Today both French and English are official languages in the country. In many areas in Canada, the French influence is still strong.

Quebec coat of arms.

GGg

is for glacier.

Glaciers are large, moving masses of ice.

They are formed when the rate of snowfall is faster than the melting rate. The unmelted snow is pressed into ice by the new snowfall. There are more than 400 glaciers in Glacier National Park in the Canadian Rockies.

H Hh

is for hockey.

British soldiers stationed in Canada developed ice hockey in the mid-1850s. Students at McGill University in Montreal, Quebec, set the rules of the game in 1879. In 1917, the major professional ice hockey league (the NHL) was formed in Montreal.

I i is for the Inuit.

The Inuit (who used to be known as Eskimos) are native inhabitants of Canada. Many Inuit live in the Nunavut territory. The First Nations (formerly known as Indians) are also native to Canada.

J j

is for Jasper National Park.

Jasper National Park is one of several national parks located in the Canadian Rockies. The Jasper Tramway is Canada's longest and highest cable car ride. It takes visitors on a ride to view six mountain ranges.

KKk

is for "kanata."

Jacques Cartier at Hochelaga (Montreal, Quebec).

"Kanata" is a Huron/ Iroquois word meaning "village." This may be where the name Canada came from. When Jacques Cartier sailed up the St. Lawrence River in 1535, he met some Iroquois and asked them what they called their land. They pointed to their village and said, "Kanata." When Cartier claimed the land for France, he called it "Canada."

L L1

is for

lumberjack.

Lumberjacks helped build Canada into the country it is today.

Almost half of Canada is covered with forests. It is one of the leading lumber producing countries in the world.

MMm

is for
maple leaf.

Maple trees were important to early Canadian settlers. They provided lumber for homes and food for families. The maple leaf is another symbol of Canada. It is displayed on the Canadian flag.

N Nn
is for
Niagara Falls.

Niagara Falls is over 12,000 years old.

The Canadian side of the falls is known as Horseshoe Falls.

Horseshoe Falls is approximately 52 meters (170 feet) high. The depth of the river at the base of the falls is estimated at 56 meters (184 feet). Millions of tourists visit Niagara Falls every year.

Oo

is for the Olympics.

Olympic Stadium in Montreal, Quebec.

Olympics • Olympics • Olympics • Olympics • Olympics • Olympics

Canada has hosted the Olympic Games twice.

Olympic Park in Montreal, Quebec, was the site of the 1976 Summer Olympics.

In 1988, the winter games were held in Calgary, Alberta.

P

Pp

is for
polar bear.

Churchill, Manitoba, is the "Polar Bear Capital of the World." The bears gather south of the town every fall. They fish in the rivers draining into Hudson Bay.

Qq

is for
Queen
Elizabeth II.

Great Britain's Queen Elizabeth II is also the Queen of Canada. She is Canada's head of state. The Queen appoints a governor-general to represent her.

R

Rr is for the **Royal Canadian Mounted Police.**

The Royal Canadian Mounted Police are the national law enforcement agency in Canada. They train in Regina, Saskatchewan.

The Mounties, as they are called, are another symbol of the country.

Ss is for stampede.

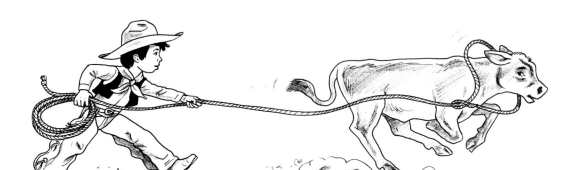

Every summer in July, Calgary hosts a livestock show and rodeo in Stampede Park. It is called the Calgary Stampede. The rodeo and show celebrate the country's cowboy heritage.

T is for the Trans-Canada Highway.

The Trans-Canada Highway is 4,857 miles long. It is the longest paved road in the world.

With its green and white maple leaf highway markers, the highway stretches from St. John, Newfoundland, to Victoria, British Columbia.

U  Uu
is for the Underground Railroad.

Many African slaves from the United States found freedom in Canada after traveling on the Underground Railroad.

The Elgin Settlement, which was the last stop on the Underground Railroad for many escaping slaves, was founded in 1849. Today the Elgin Settlement is known as Buxton. The Buxton National Historic Site and Museum can be found in North Buxton, Ontario.

A 1910 class photo on display at the Buxton Historic Site and Museum.

Vv is for Viking.

The doorway of a Viking house replica at
L'Anse-aux-Meadows National Historic Park.

Vikings settled in Newfoundland, Canada, about 1000 A.D. They called the land "Vinland." The remains of a Viking village were found at L'Anse-aux-Meadows in the 1960s.

Ww

is for
whale.

More than 30 species of whales live in or migrate through Canadian waters. Whale watching is popular on both coasts and along the St. Lawrence River in Quebec.

XXx **is for Expo '67.**

A world's fair, Expo '67, was held in Montreal to celebrate Canada's 100th birthday. Many countries built pavilions to showcase their culture. More than 50 million people from all over the world visited the fair.

Montreal's Biosphere.

Y

is for the Yukon.

YYy

In 1896, gold was discovered along the Klondike River in the Yukon.

Many people came to the region during the Gold Rush in 1898 to seek their fortunes. Most people were disappointed. Today mining is a major industry in the Yukon.

Zz is for zoo.

In addition to the wild animals living in Canada, there are also many zoos.

The Metro Toronto Zoo features over 4,000 animals from around the world. Montreal also has an insect zoo called the Insectarium!

INDEX

SUGGESTED READINGS

The author suggests the following titles to further expand a child's library on Canada:

All About Niagara Falls: Fascinating Facts, Dramatic Discoveries
  Written by Linda Granfield
  Published by Morrow
An illustrated introduction to Niagara Falls.

Canada: The Culture and Canada: The People
  Written by Bobbie Kalman
  Published by Crabtree
These nonfiction titles offer lively text and candid photographs.

Flight to Canada
  Written by Ishmael Reed
  Published by Atheneum
A look at the Underground Railroad.

The Inuksuk Book
  Written by Mary Wallace
  Published by Firefly
A fascinating look at Inuksuit, traditional Inuit stone structures that hold a special place in Inuit life and culture.

Kim Simon, former owner of the children's book wholesaler Reading Express, suggests the following titles:

Dreamstones
  Written by Maxine Trottier; Illustrated by Stella East
  Published by Stoddart Kids

Hockey (Basics for Beginners)
  Written by Laurie Wark; Illustrated by Scot Ritchie
  Published by Kids Can Press

Icebergs, Ice Caps, and Glaciers
  Written by Allan Fowler
  Published by Children's Press
A beginning reader with short text and photographs.

The Kids' Book of Canada
  Written by Barbara Greenwood; Illustrated by Jock MacRae
  Published by Kids Can Press
An illustrated guide to Canada.

REFERENCES FOR TEACHERS/PARENTS

Dino-trekking: The Ultimate Dinosaur Lover's Travel Guide
  Written by Kelly Milner Halls
  Published by Wiley

Doing Children's Museums: A Guide to 265 Hands-On Museums
  Written by Joanne Cleaver
  Published by Williamson Publications

PHOTO ACKNOWLEDGMENTS

Grateful acknowledgment is expressed to the following for permission to reprint their photographs in "C" is for Canada:

A — Jerry Kobalenko/First Light.

B — Brian Milne/First Light.

C — Ken Straiton/First Light.

D — R. Hartmier/First Light.

E — National Archives of Canada.

F — Chris Cheadle/First Light.

G — Jason Puddifoot/First Light.

H — Bernd Fuchs/First Light.

I — Bryan and Cherry Alexander/First Light.

J — Darwin Wiggett/First Light.

K — National Archives of Canada.

L — Thomas Kitchin/First Light.

M — Ron Watts/First Light.

N — D. and J. Heaton/First Light.

O — Thomas Kitchin/First Light.

P — J. Sylvester/First Light.

Q — AP/Wide World Photos.

R — Thomas Kitchin/First Light.

S — Larry J. MacDougal/First Light.

T — Patrick Morrow/First Light.

U — Courtesy of the Buxton Historic Site and Museum.

V — Wayne Wegner/First Light.

W — Victoria Hurst/First Light.

X — C. Cheadle/First Light.

Y — Patrick and Baiba Morrow/First Light.

Z — Stephen Homer/First Light.

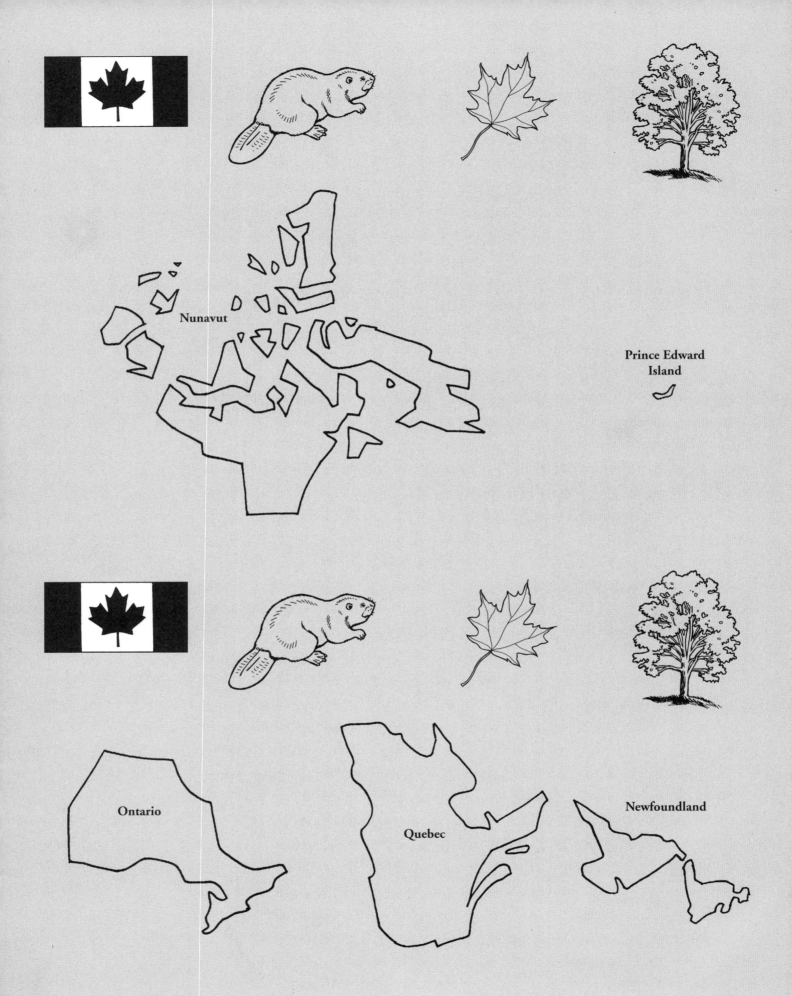

Nunavut

Prince Edward
Island

Ontario

Quebec

Newfoundland